FOLLOWING THE **Fire**

FOLLOWING THE *Fire*

DISCOVERING HOW GOD LEADS YOU BY THE DESIRES OF YOUR HEART

BY

MAC HAMMOND

Unless otherwise indicated, all Scripture quotations are taken from the *King James Version* of the Bible.

Scripture quotations marked (AMP) are taken from *The Amplified Bible, Old Testament* copyright © 1965, 1987 by The Zondervan Corporation. Those taken from *The Amplified Bible, New Testament* are copyright 1958, 1987 by the Lockman Foundation. Used by permission.

Scripture quotations marked (NKJV) are taken from the *New King James Version*. Copyright © 1979, 1980, 1982 by Thomas Nelson, Inc. Used by permission. All rights reserved.

Following the Fire—
Discovering How God Leads You
by the Desires of Your Heart

ISBN 978-1-57399-339-5

Copyright © 2007 by Mac Hammond

Published by Mac Hammond Ministries
PO Box 29469
Minneapolis, MN 55429

Printed in the United States of America. All rights reserved under International Copyright Law. Contents and/or cover may not be reproduced in whole or in part in any form without the express written consent of the publisher.

Contents

Chapter 1
Follow the Fire. 1

Chapter 2
Desire and Prayer 9

Chapter 3
Desire and Diligence 19

Chapter 4
Desire and Delight 29

Chapter 5
Desire and Delay. 39

Chapter 6
Desire and Decisions 49

Conclusion 63

CHAPTER 1

Follow the *Fire*

As a pastor, I've heard it many times and in many variations. It often starts with a complaint such as "I don't know what God wants me to do" or "I wish I knew the will of God for my life." No matter how it is expressed, it reveals one of the consistent challenges Christians face—how to discover and ultimately fulfill God's will for their individual lives.

The good news is the Bible clearly reveals a multitude of practical principles for walking out God's personal plan for each of us. As a result, this has been a frequent subject of many sermons and books. Yet even with a myriad of insightful teaching available, I still often hear and see the exasperation many sincere Christians face in this arena. Why is this the case?

I certainly don't claim to have all the answers, yet I do believe there is one aspect of how God reveals our calling to us which seems to be consistently overlooked and misunderstood. It is revealed in the answer I give when people ask me directly to help them clarify their calling. My standard reply tends to catch them by surprise. I usually say, "Friend, what desire burns in your heart?"

The instant response of most Christians is, "What do my desires have to do with it? I'm talking about the will of God here!"

Of course, there is an assumption behind that question. The assumption is that if you desire something intensely, it must not be God's will for you. God's plan must certainly be something distasteful, unpleasant, or even frightening. These presuppositions flow from a basic misunderstanding of God's nature and ways.

When we, as mature believers, get serious about seeking God's will and purpose for our lives, we tend to focus on the ministry of the Holy Spirit, which is described in the New Testament as the inner witness and the peace of God. Many of us have been taught to "follow the voice of the Spirit" or to "follow after peace."

There is a lot of wisdom in this approach. Certainly, as we make decisions, we need to seek the inward witness of the Holy Spirit and we need to follow God's peace. They are important elements of our decision-making process. They are vital parts of our lives.

However, when we talk about God's direction for our lives, our most basic consideration is desire.

The fundamental truth I want to put forth in the coming pages is that the desires of your heart can and should be a clear indicator of God's will for you.

In Scripture, we see a great illustration of this simple yet profound principle with the children of Israel. Of course, their journey toward God's will for them as a nation provides many great insights into the process of discovering and doing God's highest and best. Yet, at the core, how did the Israelites find that land of blessing and fulfillment? How did they ultimately occupy the Promised Land? They simply—*followed the fire!*

In the darkness of their wilderness journey, they followed the fire to their Land of Promise—to a land that flowed with milk and honey. Certainly, there were battles to be fought, issues to address, and obstacles to overcome. Yet following the fire is what led them toward their destiny. And the same is true for us.

In the same way, for you to successfully occupy your God-ordained place in the body of Christ, you must learn to follow the fire of desire that burns in your heart. To me, this is the most basic truth regarding the leadership of the Holy Spirit and the process God has established for influencing your decisions, direction, and thus destiny.

Your Unique God-Given Fire

As we begin our study, I want you to begin looking at the biblical symbol of "the fire" a little differently than it has routinely been preached in the body of Christ. Usually what you hear is an exhortation: "You need to be on fire for Jesus." The implication is that somehow you can light your own fire simply by an act of your will. That isn't the case, however.

The Word tells us that Jesus is the one who baptizes us with the Holy Spirit, but Jesus doesn't stop there. He also baptizes with fire. When you receive the Holy Spirit, you also receive the fire of God (Matthew 3:11).

Obviously, this doesn't refer to a literal fire burning. Throughout the New Testament, the fire of God is best defined as fervency or zeal. Zeal can be defined as vehement desire (see 2 Corinthians 7:11).

So when we talk about fire, we're essentially talking about desire. The things you most strongly desire are the things you burn about. Those are the things you can fan the flames of and become intensely fervent about.

These desires indicate the specific direction of God for your life. It shows you where He wants you to go.

What did the children of Israel do in the darkness of their wilderness journey? They followed the fire. Where did the fire take them? It took them to their Land of Promise, a land that flowed with milk and honey.

You have a Land of Promise waiting for you—a place filled with amazing things that eye hasn't seen and ear hasn't heard (1 Corinthians 2:9). Every believer has a Land of Promise to walk in, a life available to them now. True, you'll need to fight some giants and scale some walled cities, just as the Israelites did. But God says He has given you the land. You simply need to obediently follow the fire.

The Word makes it clear that Jesus has already lit a fire in our hearts. Fire is already burning within you. God has put a fire in you that you are to follow. Now there are certainly things you can do to dampen the flames and cause the fire to burn not as brightly, but God is the one who has put a type of fire in you that is unlike that of any other believer!

And you're not to burn like somebody else burns. Everybody's burning for something different. You need to learn to fan the flames of your own fire and then follow that fire.

Yet, typically, we have certain Christians who we greatly admire and thus decide we're going to try to burn like they're burning, desire passionately what they desire. This is a common stumbling block. And, in reality, it is a dangerous deception, because you yourself cannot decide what you want to be on fire for. You can only determine the unique fire God has given you and then follow it!

For example, I have a friend in ministry who is on fire for the nation of Israel. She burns intensely for the prophetic destiny of that land. I love her for that, but do you know what I discovered? I can't burn the same way she does.

Clearly, I have a heart for Israel as all Christians should. According to the Bible, the nation of Israel and the Jewish people occupy a prominent place in the plan of God and it is important to be actively involved in blessing them. But I simply don't burn as brightly or in the same manner she does on these issues, as this "fire" shapes her calling and defines God's will for her life.

Likewise, I don't seem to burn for the nations around the world as some believers do. Of course, I certainly appreciate the need to be missions minded and I am actively involved in getting the Good News of the Gospel into every corner of the globe. But because the call of God on my life is that of a local pastor, my greatest desire is for my city. And as long as darkness permeates the community that I'm a part of, I see my principle responsibility being there. That's how I burn.

I have a fire that is directly related to the call God has put in my heart. And the same is true for you. You have a call that is unique to your particular collection of gifts, talents, and abilities. That is the only way you can burn. If you try to burn like somebody else is burning, it simply isn't going to work.

If you begin to compare yourself with others or follow someone else's fire, you will start thinking, "I must be unspiritual. I wonder what's wrong with me. Look how they're on fire for that cause. I just must be a carnal old do-nothing."

Herein is truth: anything that's going to work for you in the kingdom of God as it's supposed to work is going to have to be born out of the unique fire God has placed in your heart.

Thus, it is important to identify this type of thinking and not allow it to infiltrate your pursuit of God, as every believer is different. Let God bring out the uniqueness of what He has called you to do instead of comparing yourself to others.

How to do just that is our focus in the following chapters. We will look at the power of desire and how you can take significant steps toward your divine destiny by learning how to figure out, focus on, and add fuel to your fire of desire so you can follow it to your Promised Land!

CHAPTER 2

DESIRE AND Prayer

Have you noticed throughout the record of Scripture and history, the people who have experienced great manifestations of God's grace and glory have been praying people? From their experiences, we can ascertain that a lifestyle of prayer will create a spiritual atmosphere in which great things are accomplished in the plans and purposes of God.

Yet, the kind of powerful prayer and heart cry that seems to consistently bring God on the scene can't be something you just engage in as "Ho-hum, guess I'll pray in agreement with the rest of the body tonight." No. Forget it. It has to be born out of a deep desire, as this is always true about effective prayer.

When supernatural things happen, you will discover that the people involved were simply following the fire of desire in their hearts and were so hungry for God that they were unwilling for their desire to be denied.

How important is desire to effective prayer? Friend, you can't even pray the prayer of faith without it. Notice the use of the word "desire" in the familiar phrases of Mark 11:24, 25:

> *Therefore I say unto you, What things soever ye desire, when ye pray, believe that ye receive them, and ye shall have them. And when ye stand praying, forgive, if ye have ought against any: that your Father also which is in heaven may forgive you your trespasses.*

Notice that it doesn't say whatsoever things your *wife* desires, your *pastor* desires, or, whatsoever things you *think you ought to have*. No. It is whatsoever things *you* desire.

For many years, I have heard teachings about Mark 11:24 that emphasize the importance of believing when you pray. However, I haven't heard much teaching about the significance of desire. And yet, desire gives your prayer the intensity that makes it a fervent, effectual prayer.

I used to pray for a litany of things that were not in my heart and I had no burning desire for them. My religious training taught me that a good Christian was obligated to pray for those things. However, without desire, my prayers were the empty, vain repetitions that Matthew 6:7 talks about. They didn't go anywhere.

The spiritual principle is that desire is an absolutely necessary ingredient for effective prayer. Want more evidence? Let's look at James 5:16 which starts off by saying, "Confess your faults one to another, and pray one for another, that ye may be healed." This sentence tells us that prayer is the subject. Then it makes this statement: "The effectual fervent prayer of a righteous man availeth much."

Many read this passage and get hung up on the righteous part. Let me remind you that if you're born again, you've been made the righteousness of God in Christ Jesus. You qualify to pray an effective prayer!

The Amplified Bible says it this way: "The earnest (heartfelt, continued) prayer of a righteous man makes tremendous power available [dynamic in its working]."

Effective prayer is not a casual experience. It is a prayer that comes from deep within, and it has to be continual. It is a prayer that is born out of undeniable, insatiable hunger and deep, fervent desire. All of your spiritual energy needs to be wrapped up in your cry.

Clarifying your calling and fulfilling your God-given destiny can't be your third desire or your second desire. It has to become the most important desire in your life. It needs to be the paramount desire, the supreme desire of your soul.

There is something in the call of the soul that is creative. It brings things to pass. When you cry out to God, His creative power begins to focus on the thing that you are praying about. Your faith blends with His power to become a creative exercise.

You get His presence on you. You begin to see His hand at work. You begin to work together with God to evidence the creative power of desire. If desire is not present, it's not going to be an effectual prayer. It's not going to be a powerful prayer. It won't bring any power to bear to change the circumstance.

Keep on Keeping It Before You

Prayer, to be effective, also has to be persistent. In Luke 18:1-8, in the parable of the persistent widow, God makes it clear that we need to "cry out day and night," like the widow who came back to the unjust judge again and again. Luke 11:9-13 tells us to keep knocking, seeking, and asking until our desires are given to us, and that's what we need to do.

I've discovered in my own prayer life, in order to remain passionate about what God has called me to do, I've got to keep it before me. The best time to do that is in my time with the Lord. I dwell upon it and think about it. This is the way you intensify your desire and your passion for something by seeing yourself walking in it.

You can't "think up" God's plan for your life. You can't use your reasoning capacity or your education to figure out the blessings that God has planned for you.

According to 1 Corinthians 2:9, "Eye hath not seen, nor ear heard, neither have entered into the heart of man the things which God hath prepared for them that love him." However, verse 10 says that God will reveal these things to you by His Spirit. As the things that you could not have thought of or asked for unfold in your life, they will not always come to you as a complete shock or total surprise. God will prepare you to receive them and will unveil them to you.

First Corinthians 2:13 in *The Amplified Bible* says, "And we are setting these truths forth in words not taught by human wisdom but taught by the [Holy] Spirit, combining and interpreting spiritual truths with spiritual language [to those who possess the Holy Spirit]."

If you want to receive "exceedingly, abundantly, above all that you ask or think," your first step of preparation is to be filled with the Holy Spirit and then using the Holy Spirit as your guide, you must pray out the will of God for your life.

The Priority of Personal Prayer

Prayer is the first place to begin to find, form, and fuel the fire of desire within your heart which will lead toward fulfilling your destiny. It is really not complicated or difficult, yet it is important to recognize it is something *you* must do yourself.

Over the years, you can't imagine the numbers of people that call on my wife to pray about the will of God for their lives. No, the first place you begin to form and fuel the fire of godly desire is through your own personal prayer life.

When you pray, I want you to overcome the tendency to look for a vision or some spectacular sign. "Oh, to see a burning bush or handwriting on the wall!" Instead, start paying attention to the desires that form in your heart and look at them as God's response to your prayers.

It is easy to ignore this arena because we think that our desires are rooted in self-interest, so they must not be God. In fact, most Christians mistrust their desires. I have heard people say, "You have to be careful about where your desires take you."

"I have the desire to make money for the Gospel," a businessman might say. "I want to build a company that pours millions of dollars into the kingdom of God." But to him, that can't be a God-given desire. It must be a selfish, carnal desire. "It must be a desire of *my flesh*." The religious teaching he has received causes him to discount the desire to create wealth.

"I have a desire to become a school board member," a housewife might say. "I want to sit in front of my neighbors at a school board meeting and make godly decisions that benefit the children in my community. But I know that this is a silly, carnal desire. I must be on a power trip. This desire could not have come from the Lord." And so she dismisses the desire.

DESIRE: A SOURCE OF SUCCESS

Certainly, the enemy of your soul wants to pervert and corrupt your desires. He labors to turn the godly force of desire into the ungodly forces of lust, covetousness, envy, selfishness, and jealousy. Yes, Christians can certainly be pulled away from the Lord and begin to have ungodly desires which can easily be recognized by their selfish nature.

Yet, for now, I want you to recognize the common tendency when we pray is to over-spiritualize and not pay any attention to the desires which begin to ignite in our hearts, even though we can clearly see that desire is often the basis for success elsewhere.

For example, the men and women who go the furthest in business are the ones who have the greatest desire to succeed. The ones who are so single-minded and hungry for success that they are willing to make any necessary sacrifice are the ones who make it to the top. They are willing to "pay the price" and "go the second mile."

The same thing is true in the world of sports, where it has become a cliché to say that the guy who wins the game is the one who wants it the most. When talent, ability, and skill levels are similar, the team that wins the game is the team that has the greatest desire to win.

For example, before a professional football game, commentators often say, "These teams are evenly matched, but I think that Team A will win the game because they really want the victory. They are hungrier."

God-Given Desire

Desire is not simply a natural truth. It is not merely the way that professional sports and the corporate world operate. It is part of God's process for clarifying our calling and leading us to our Promised Land.

Desire and Prayer

Without desire, we will never make it to our appointment with destiny. It is the element that has to be present. But Philippians 2:13 shows us that God creates the desire that we need. The verse in the King James translation says, "For it is God which worketh in you both to will and to do of his good pleasure."

The Wuest translation says, "God is the one who is constantly putting forth his energy in you both in the form of your being desirous of and your doing his good pleasure."

Listen to what *The Way* translation says: "It is God who is all the while supplying the impulse, giving you the power to resolve and the strength to perform the execution of his good pleasure."

In other words, it is God Himself who gives you the desire to do His will. It is God Himself who gives you the hunger to reach your appointment with destiny. He creates the impulse, the energy, the strength, and the resolve. He initiates the desire.

So as you begin to pray about God's plans and purposes for your life, remember that one of the primary ways God reveals His will to you is through the desires that He plants in your heart. Begin to pay attention to and follow the fires that begin to burn!

Chapter 3

Desire and *Diligence*

Because of our unregenerate, carnal nature, our natural tendency is to be self-centered. If we don't reign in our carnal nature and we just allow things to happen haphazardly, without plan or direction, we will not desire God. We will not have a hunger for Him, and we will not seek or serve Him. We will serve the cravings of our flesh, which are self-gratifying desires.

Thus, we are faced with a dilemma. If we want to open our lives to godly desires, we need to cultivate a desire for God. We need to cultivate a hunger for Him. If we fail to do that, we cannot trust the desires that come, because they will be born of the flesh and thus selfish in nature.

However, desiring God is not something that happens automatically in our lives. Because we live in a carnal body that has natural desires, desiring God is not always something that comes easily. How do we ignite our desire for God so serving Him becomes a joy and not a duty? The answer is revealed in Hebrews 11:6:

> *But without faith it is impossible to please him: for he that cometh to God must believe that he is, and that he is a rewarder of them that diligently seek him.*

This verse reveals a process we must go through to increase our desire for God. It begins by revealing that the only way we can live successfully in this life is by faith. It says, "But without faith it is impossible to please Him."

And then it gives us a definition of the faith that pleases God. "For he that cometh to God must believe that He is and that He is a rewarder of them that diligently seek Him."

We see from this verse that faith has two parts. The first part of faith is very basic. We must believe that God exists. We must believe that He is. The second part of faith is the part that a lot of people miss, but it is the part that connects faith with desire.

We must believe that He is a rewarder of those who diligently seek Him. A reward is always definable in terms of fulfilled desire. Faith believes that God will fulfill the desires of those who diligently seek Him. Rewards are faith's connection with desire.

Run for the Rewards

The Bible talks a lot about rewards. Jesus often promises us that God will reward us for being doers of the Word. We see after the Rapture of the Church, we will stand before the judgment seat of Christ and experience the handing out of rewards for the deeds we did while we were living on earth in this body.

Rewards will be given, and we know a reward, by definition, is a fulfilled desire. We also know that God is not going to fulfill a carnal desire. He is not going to grant you a desire that is rooted in your flesh or is based on self-gratification. The only desire God can fulfill is a godly desire.

The implication then is that the rewards will be given to people who have delighted themselves in the Lord and have committed themselves to Him. The suggestion is that the rewards will be given to those who have aligned their lives with God's Word and have received His desires in their hearts. If He is your first desire, then experiencing Him will be your first eternal reward.

After the Rapture of the Church, we will experience the fullness of His presence in a literal sense. Certainly, this is a big part of our reward.

We will also enjoy the fulfillment of all the experiences that He wanted to provide for us on earth but was unable to give us because of mistakes.

In our flesh, we sometimes do wrong things and miss things that God wanted to give us in this earthly experience. We really want something, but the desire is not fulfilled.

It may be a family relationship that went sour. It may be a marriage that was not fulfilling. It may be an unsuccessful job. It could be a lot of things. In this life, we sometimes miss it.

However, if we have conducted our lives on the basis of the Word, and if we have walked in love with other people as well as we know how, then there will be a reward in the eternal realm. Even if we miss it on earth, we will experience it there.

However, we also receive rewards while we are still living in this body on earth. We receive rewards for reaching the marks of God's plan for our lives. There are prizes and rewards for reaching the high calling of God.

All of these rewards come to us when we diligently seek God and cultivate a hunger and desire for Him that is greater than any other desire that we have.

He said that He will reward you if you diligently seek Him. This is the way you begin to be rewarded with the experience of His presence and the manifestation of His person, His power, and His glory in your life. Diligently seeking Him will expand the desire for Him in your soul, and your desire for Him will properly orient your life.

When you don't feel like getting up early, get up early anyway. Drag your flesh out of bed even if it wants to sleep for another hour, so you can read the Bible and pray. When you need to catch up with your work at home and don't feel like getting dressed and going to church, go to church anyway. Make sure you go to church Sunday morning, Sunday night, and Wednesday night, every time the doors are open, even if it is inconvenient.

This is what it means to be a diligent seeker of God. This is where the life of faith begins. This is where rewards begin. This is where your desire for God will grow. This is how duty turns into delight.

Desire and Faith

Of course, you must exercise your faith. You must believe that if you are a diligent seeker of God, He will reward you. Otherwise, the effort will be lost.

In fact, this is where faith and desire work together. Diligently seek Him in faith, believing He will reward your faithful diligence with an experience of His presence and a desire for Him that you would not otherwise have. Continue to seek Him and cultivate a desire for Him, even when doubts, challenges, and moments of uncertainty come. Keep Him in first place in your life, believing the desires that come are an outline of His will for your life, and pursue the desires that come. Believe that He will fulfill those desires.

I don't care what it is. If you have a desire to be a millionaire and you know that it is not rooted in selfishness but is a desire to be used by God to promote the Gospel in this world, then pursue that desire diligently and believe that it will be fulfilled.

He will reward you with the fulfillment of your desire. He will reward you with experiences of His presence and His love. And all of this emanates from being a diligent seeker of God.

This is the outline for the way to succeed in the kingdom of God. Desire is where the will of God begins to be revealed, and desire is where rewards begin to come. But only for those who diligently seek Him.

If you are not a diligent seeker of God, you cannot trust your desires. They may come from the flesh, and you may be deceived.

However, if you are a diligent seeker of God, you can trust the desires that come.

QUESTIONING YOUR DESIRE

As we've seen, my basic thesis is this: if you are diligently seeking God, the desires that are born in your heart will be of Him. Once you recognize that truth, you simply exercise your faith and believe you will be rewarded with the fulfillment of those desires. This is the central theme of faith.

For me, this is a meaningful spiritual truth because it is relevant to the past and present experiences of my own life.

Many times, unknowingly, I have questioned the rightness of my desires. I've said, "This doesn't fit with my natural understanding. This doesn't seem to be something that should be a priority in my life. This doesn't seem to have ministry value. I don't think God would be interested in this." I have found myself saying these things as I examined the desires of my heart.

However, after God showed me the truth about desire, I began to manage the desires of my heart in a different way. I knew that God was in first place in my life. I knew that I was delighting myself in Him and diligently seeking Him, so I stopped saying, "This desire must be rooted in self-interest." I began to trust my desires. I began to exercise my faith to believe that they were God-given desires sponsored by the Holy Spirit.

Even when I couldn't understand them intellectually and even when they didn't seem to fit into the larger scheme of things, I began to follow the desires of my heart and to believe they were a revelation of God's will for my life. I began to trust God to bring them to pass.

Perhaps, without even noticing or thinking about it, you have also questioned your desires. Perhaps you've said, "Surely I made this one up. This one must be rooted in self-interest. This one cannot possibly be from the Lord."

If you are diligently seeking God and if He is your chief desire, the desires you feel are from Him. He authored those desires. Even if you can't intellectually understand them, you can be assured they are a revelation of God's will for your life.

If this is not your approach, the desires God places in your heart will be squelched. Many Christians consistently do this because even though they know their desires should be for the Lord, they believe that any other hopes and dreams are inappropriate.

For example, I talk to a lot of single people who suppress the desire to be married because they believe that their only desire should be to serve God. "I will just desire the Lord and let Him deal with my marriage problem," they say.

So they push down the desire that would cause the marriage to manifest even though the apostle Paul makes it clear that by the will of God there are very few celibates. God's purpose is that most people be married. So if you are a single person who is serving God and desires to be married, you can be assured God gave you that desire and wants it to grow in your life.

Pray about it. Ask God to stir it in you. Many people hesitate to fuel the desire for a marriage partner. Deep down, some people shy away from the sacrifice and commitment that marriage requires. If you have a desire to be in a godly marriage, then you need to allow that desire to become a burning fire and you need to become fervent about the benefits of a godly marriage. When you do, God will begin to paint a picture in your heart of the general qualifications you should look for in an appropriate marriage partner. And the result will be a godly marriage.

SEEK AND GODLY DESIRE WILL COME

If you are diligently seeking God and if He is your chief desire, the desires you feel are from Him. He authored those desires. Even if you can't intellectually understand them, you can be assured they are a revelation of God's will for your life.

I encourage you to follow your desires. Believe that as you cultivate a desire for God and diligently seek Him, He will reward you by fulfilling your desires. If you have God in the right place in your life, then it is appropriate that you pursue and believe for the fulfillment of your desires. In fact, if you want to live a life of faith and succeed in the kingdom of God, it is mandatory that you operate this way.

CHAPTER 4

DESIRE AND *Delight*

A key verse in our study on the power of desire and the role it plays in leading you toward the will of God for your life is Psalm 37:4: "Delight thyself also in the Lord; and he shall give thee the desires of thine heart."

This verse has two applications or can be accurately interpreted in two different ways. First, when you delight yourself in the Lord, He will fulfill the desires that currently reside in your heart. This is the typical view of this verse and it certainly is true that God honors those who honor Him. Or as is often said, you focus on God's dream and He will focus on yours.

Yet a little deeper look reveals that if God is your first priority and if you find your joy and pleasure in Him, He will be the one who authors your desires and places them in your heart. He will ignite a particular fire on the inside of you that when followed, will light the way to your calling.

In both cases, the understood subject is *you* and the key word is *delight*. Your part is to delight yourself in the Lord. God's part is to fulfill current right desires and impart desires into your heart that are aligned with His purpose and plan for your life.

So the word "delight" is revealed as a primary key to opening our lives to the direction God gives and intensifying right desire. Thus, understanding its meaning and integrating it into our lives becomes paramount.

Literally in the Hebrew, the word *delight* means: "take your pleasure in or find your joy in the Lord." Of course, prayer is a foundational part of the outworking of "delight" and certainly an element of delight can be found in praise and worship. Both of these arenas are how this verse is typically taught and applied.

Yet *delight* when properly understood has a more comprehensive application; in fact, it means to make God the number one consideration in your life. Take more pleasure in God than you do your wife, your husband, your children, or your vocation. Take more pleasure in God than you do anything else. Keep God at the top of your priorities' list. In other words, we must make Him our heart's desire, our first love, and our source of joy.

Delighting in God means we want to know more about Him. It means we want to know Him in a deeper, more personal way. It means we hunger for His presence and His person and want to be in intimate fellowship with Him. It means we seek, or go after, Him.

DELIGHT IN MEN AND WOMEN OF SCRIPTURE

As we go through the Bible, we notice that many successful men and women of Scripture definitely took their delight in God. As we study their lives, we are able to feel the heat of their passion for Him and see the victories they experienced as a result.

For example, in Psalm 143:6, David says, "I stretch forth my hands unto thee: my soul thirsteth after thee, as a thirsty land."

In other words, David had delighted in the Lord to the point he had cultivated a passionate desire for God. His prayers are as intense as the cries of a thirsty man who is in the midst of a famine and desperately cries out for rain.

In Psalm 119:20, Ezra says, "My soul breaks with longing for Your judgments at all times" (NKJV). The New Living translation says, "I am overwhelmed continually with a desire for Your laws."

Years ago, I studied Paul's life. I realized the most interesting thing about him was that he was a zealous man. Everything about him was intense. Throughout the New Testament, he made passionate statements: "I long after this" or "I yearn for this." He used dramatic, expressive words to define the intensity of his fervor.

The world will make you indifferent. The flesh will make you spiritually cold. However, if you commit to God, make Him your priority, and keep your mind set upon Him, your fire will begin to burn brighter. The fact is when we delight in Him and draw closer to Him, He puts intense desire in our hearts and our fervency grows.

A great example of what begins to happen is found in Mark 10:46-52, the story about Jesus healing a blind man named Bartimaeus.

> *And they came to Jericho. And as He went out of Jericho with His disciples and a great multitude, blind Bartemaeus, the son of Timaeus, sat by the roadside begging. And when he heard that it was Jesus of Nazareth, he began to cry out…* (NKJV).

One translation says, "He began to scream for all he was worth, shouting, 'Jesus, have pity and mercy on me.' And many severely censored and reproved him, telling him to keep still, but he kept on shouting out all the more." Another translation says that he cried out all the louder.

I like Bartemaeus' fervency; he was not casual about being healed. He had an intense desire. Even though Jesus was in a great crowd, He heard Bartimaeus' cry. He stopped and said, "Call him."

The disciples and others in the crowd called the blind man, telling him, "Take courage. Get up," and Bartimaeus leapt up.

In those days, people wore cloaks if they had afflictions or maladies. These cloaks identified their infirmities. When Jesus called him, Bartimaeus threw off his cloak. When he came to Jesus, he probably used a cane or leaned on someone's arm, but he already knew that blindness was leaving him. There is something about fervency that causes it to mix well with faith.

In Mark 10:51–52, Jesus said to Bartimaeus, "'What do you want Me to do for you?' Bartimaeus said, 'Master, let me receive my sight.' And Jesus said, 'Go your way; your faith has healed you'" (AMP).

I think that Jesus' question is very interesting because it illustrates the spiritual truth that God can't do things among men simply because He wants to. First, He has to find a man who wants those things as fervently as He wants them. On the other hand, God can do anything on earth if He can find a man who wants it as much as He does.

DELIGHT = COMMITMENT

We see delighting in the Lord was a key element in the lives of spiritually successful people, so let's be sure we understand the totality of what it means. To further illuminate the meaning of this key concept, let's look to Psalm 37:5 which says, "Commit thy way unto the Lord; trust also in Him, and he shall bring it to pass."

The subject has not changed from the preceding verse. We are still talking about delight and desire. However, the wording has changed. We see the Bible's definition for "delighting yourself in the Lord" in the next verse is the phrase, "committing your way unto Him." In other words, committing your way unto the Lord is synonymous with delighting in Him.

When you commit your way to the Lord, you make every area of your life available to Him. His Word and His purpose for your life become of utmost importance to you. You use every resource and make every effort to commit your way unto Him. You focus your attention on Him. He is your top priority and you are delighting in Him.

You remember Psalm 1 which talks about the man who prospers in anything that he sets his hand to? It says, "His delight is in the law of the Lord, and in his law doth he meditate day and night." Psalm 1:2 says that God's leading comes to those who are delighting themselves in His law and thinking about it day and night. This means that *delight* also involves what you focus your mind upon.

This is not hard to grasp; for when you're committed to or delighting in something or someone, you think about them, don't you? If you're committed to flying and are delighting yourself in it, you think about the joy of doing loops and rolls and clover leafs and Cuban 8s and all the different things that represent how flying can be a blessing to you.

DELIGHT INVOLVES OUR THOUGHT LIVES

When we delight ourselves in something, we think about it all the time. When we delight in God, His desires begin to occupy our thought lives, and we focus our thoughts on His Word. We may be focusing our thoughts on a promise we have found in the Bible, or we may be thinking about something He has spoken to us about our individual lives: an idea that He has given us, His person, what eternity might hold. All of these things are ways of delighting in the Lord.

Obviously, there are times when our thoughts are focused on the daily tasks we have to do. There may be other times when our thoughts are misdirected and introverted and begin to minister to the desires of self.

During those times, we need to guard ourselves against the desires that come. However, when we focus our discretionary thought time on the things of God and His Word, we are delighting in the Lord and we can trust the desires that begin to burn brighter as we do.

Isaiah 55:8-9 sheds even more light on this where it says, "For my thoughts are not your thoughts, neither are your ways my ways, saith the Lord. For as the heavens are higher than the earth, so are my ways higher than your ways, and my thoughts than your thoughts."

As we have seen, you cannot delight in something and birth desire for it without thinking about it. Thus, this passage shows us that when our minds are filled with the carnal thoughts of our flesh, we live on a low plane and a small life. We have no fervor for God.

However, when we are born again, we gain access to God's thoughts. First Corinthians 2:16 says we are now able to possess the mind of Christ. One of the first things God asks us to do is to renew our minds. He wants us to take His thoughts so we can begin to think the way He thinks.

For example, the carnal mind says, "God is a judging God. Don't expect very much help from Him." If we take the mind of Christ and if we receive the thoughts of God, they cause us to realize that God wants to bless and multiply our lives.

God's thoughts are as high as heaven. If we begin to think God's thoughts instead of our flesh's thoughts, we will begin to walk in a higher realm. In fact, God's thoughts are like containers, and they contain the spark, or seed, of desire. When we take His thoughts, we also take His desire. As we begin to think as He thinks, we also begin to desire His plans.

This is the place where a lot of people miss God's higher life. They receive the thought and with the thought comes desire, but they don't stir and cultivate the desire. Often, they don't even talk about it very much. Instead, they neglect the desire, or they hold it casually, and it dies away.

Desire is like a seed that has been dropped into your soul. If you care for the seed, it begins to grow. You begin to ask God to cause the seed to grow. You talk to Him about the desire, it will become increasingly stronger.

STIR THE FIRE

The bottom line is that you can't delight yourself in something you don't commit to and think about. So an important understanding we must have is "to delight in the Lord" which means to be committed to fill our minds with God's thoughts and ways as revealed by the written Word and the Holy Spirit.

As you do, the desires that begin to spring up in you are born of the Holy Spirit and have come to you from the Lord. You can be assured that your desires are God given and are a revelation of His will and purpose for your life. So make a decision now to make delighting in Him a significant part of your daily life!

Remember, desire is like a fire. And like a literal fire, if we don't stir it and stoke it, it dies down. When the fire in a fireplace begins to die down, we use a poker to stir the fire so that it will blaze again. In a spiritual sense, delight is the poker that keeps the fire of desire blazing and growing in our lives.

Chapter 5

Desire and *Delay*

No one likes to wait. All of us are impatient to some degree. Some of us more than others, of course. When we begin to get glimpses of the wonderful things God wants to bring to us and a desire to pursue them, waiting on the fulfillment of His word can be tough, especially when the complete fulfillment does not come as quickly as we had hoped.

During those times, we ask ourselves, "Why is this taking so long?" We are in the place between seeing the promise and receiving it and this can be a challenging place. I have heard it called "God's waiting room."

We usually arrive in the waiting room immediately after receiving illumination, revelation, or a vision—three closely related levels of spiritual experience.

Illumination, although an operation of the Holy Spirit, affects the mental realm. It is the moment when a portion of the Word becomes clear to your understanding.

For example, you may be reading a portion of the Bible that you have read many times before and the Holy Spirit illuminates it for you. All at once, you see something in the Word you have never seen before.

You may be at church, hearing the preaching of the Word. Perhaps you have been a believer for a long time and have heard a dozen sermons on a certain spiritual topic, but a guest speaker brings it to you under a different anointing and illuminates things you have never understood before.

Illumination brings understanding about something that already has been communicated. Revelation, which is closely related to illumination, reveals things that have not been written anywhere and you have not thought about before. Revelation is the moment when you receive godly concepts and ideas that "eye hasn't seen and ear hasn't heard."

Revelation is very exciting. You may be sitting in your prayer closet enjoying the presence of God when He begins to reveal new things to you, and the experience is like an explosion.

Perhaps the highest level of spiritual experience is a vision. Occasionally, people will talk with Jesus during these experiences, or they will be caught up into a particular spiritual place. Time seems to be suspended, and ten hours seem like ten minutes. Acts 10:10 describes the experience as a trance.

During visions, people often see the fulfillment of things they have been praying about or that God has promised them. They receive new dreams and ideas. Things come alive in their hearts, and their minds are opened to new areas of understanding regarding God's intentions and plans.

God's Waiting Room

Spiritual encounters have a way of changing your life. Every time you have an encounter with the Holy Spirit, whether from reading the Word or through revelation or vision, you get hungry for the things God is showing you.

Desire is birthed in your heart, and the intensity of the desire is relative to the type of spiritual experience you have. Yet no matter how it comes or how strong it is, once desire is birthed, you are in the Lord's waiting room. You are in the midst of experiencing delayed fulfillment of divine desire.

Of course, everyone is experiencing delayed desire in some area of his or her life. People in wheelchairs get illumination about healing, and they wait to be healed. Parents get illumination about God's plans for their children and yet must wait for God's plans to materialize. When God gives you a promise about your marriage or your business, you are in the waiting room until the promise manifests.

You may be tempted to say, "How long are you going to make me wait, Lord? Why are you doing this to me?" However, it is vital to recognize your own behavior and way of relating to God often determines how long you are in the waiting room. Almost invariably, the delay in the manifestation of His promises is the result of the need for further preparation in our lives.

WAITING-ROOM WISDOM

When we find ourselves experiencing delayed desire, trust is the most essential element of successful waiting. In fact, we frequently stay in the waiting room longer than we would like to stay because we don't have a sufficient amount of trust.

Instead of getting restless and trying to figure out how to accomplish God's work in your own strength, you need to settle down and trust that God knows best. You need to come to the place of acknowledging that God knows more about your needs than you do and that you are where you need to be. Remind yourself that He knows how to fulfill the desires He has birthed in your heart and He really does not need your wisdom, help, or advice.

When you find yourself in God's waiting room, another important lesson is to consider your ways. This spiritual instruction is given to us in Haggai 1:5, where God says, "Now therefore thus saith the Lord of hosts; Consider your ways." One of the reasons for God's waiting room is so we can examine our lives. And when we do, Scripture tells us to look closely at two areas.

The first area is our priorities. According to Haggai 1, our first priority needs to be building the house of God. If we build our own house and look after ourselves while God's house lies in ruins, and if we put our personal agenda above God's plan, we will be like men who put on layers and layers of clothing but never get warm inside. We won't be empowered or satisfied. Our first priority needs to be expanding God's house, or His kingdom, and aligning our lives with God's plans and purposes.

The second area we need to consider is the area of faith. Second Corinthians 13:5 says, "Examine yourselves, whether ye be in the faith." When our prayers are not being answered and life is not going our way, our tendency is to test and prove Christ and to question Him. But this verse instructs us to examine ourselves, and we examine our own lives on the basis of the fruit that we produce.

We are unable to produce good fruit if we are not living by faith and delighting in Him. If we examine our lives and realize we do not have an abundance of love, peace, joy, patience, longsuffering, gentleness, goodness, and faith, and if we realize that our relationships are not undergirded by the love of God, then we can be assured we are not ready to leave God's waiting room.

Appointed Times

Another important understanding to have while in the waiting room is the difference between promises that are available to you when you exercise your faith and promises that only come at a time the Bible describes as "the appointed time."

In order to gain understanding about the appointed time, let's look at a familiar Bible passage. Habakkuk 2:2-3 says, "Write the vision, and make it plain upon tables, that he may run that readeth it. For the vision is yet for an appointed time, but at the end it shall speak, and not lie: though it tarry, wait for it; because it will surely come, it will not tarry."

Habakkuk 2:3 seems contradictory as it says, "Though it tarry … it will not tarry." But

Desire and Delay

if we study the original Hebrew words, the verse reads this way: "Though it seems to be delayed, wait for it because it will surely come. It will not be late." Habakkuk 2:3 describes the events in our lives that have an appointed time. Those things will only come at the time God has chosen, no matter what we do.

Most of the things that represent God's will for your individual life do not have an appointed time. For example, there is no timing about God's will to heal you. Two thousand years ago, your healing was secured by the stripes and suffering of Jesus and has no appointed time. When you align yourself with God's Word, your healing comes.

God's financial blessing has no appointed time. It is a promise of God that is available to all believers and can be appropriated by faith.

With few exceptions, the events that have an appointed time are the things that impact larger numbers of people and are part of God's overall redemptive plan. They usually involve God's high call on our lives, our interaction with other members of the body of Christ, and our place in the corporate effort of the Church.

For example, the Bible says that Jesus came at an appointed time. The New Testament's terminology is "the fullness of time." God planned a specific time for Jesus to come to earth and no amount of prayer or exercise of faith could alter His arrival time. There was a fullness of time that had to be reached before Jesus could come.

In your personal life, the will of God is always available to you. Whenever you get to a place of faith in your walk with Him and are able to receive His promises, He shows you His plan for your life.

The appointed time works differently. God wants to include you in His larger redemptive plan, but His plan moves forward whether you embrace it or not. The implication of Scripture is that you can miss God's appointed time if you don't give it a place in your life, which is a chilling thought.

We see this with the scribes and Pharisees, who missed their divine appointment with Jesus Christ. God gave them sufficient revelation about the coming of the Messiah, and when Jesus stood among them, they should have known that He was the Christ. However, their counterfeit religion numbed them to the presence of God's Spirit, and they missed their time of visitation with the King. Their lives changed eternally.

Our divine appointments are the most significant considerations of our lives. On a daily basis, by faith, we need to prepare ourselves for our encounters with destiny.

How do we do that? Habakkuk 2:2-3 identifies what we can do to position ourselves properly.

Preparation for the Appointed Time

Habakkuk 2:2 says that the vision needs to be made "plain on tablets that he may run who readeth it" (NKJV).

In other words, you need to write down the things that God reveals to you. The writing process produces clarity, so if you take the time to put the things God has shown you into writing, you will have a deeper understanding of them. Writing them down will help you make them plain and clear, and clarity is the essential element in momentum, which is the ability to "run."

If we don't understand something, we won't pursue it. But we have a tendency to run toward those things we clearly understand. Running produces momentum, and momentum positions us to receive our appointment with destiny.

I have made it a practice to write down the things God has shown me. I often also describe them to other groups of people. As I have thought about these things and talked about them, they have become clear and very real to me. As a result, I am able to pursue them with determination and intensity. And each time I go over them again, I grow more intense in my desire to see them manifest.

Once again, desire is the key element in all of this. God has used desire to order my steps and bring direction to my life. Desire has been God's way of taking me toward my appointment with destiny.

Write It and Run

When God brings you illumination, revelation, or vision, you need to write down what He has shown you and take steps to elevate the intensity of your desire for it. Even if the things He shows you are so big that they seem impossible, you need to develop a desire for them.

If you are experiencing discouragement as a result of delay, apply the lessons we have learned about the waiting room. Check your priorities, examine your faith, and be sure you're not trying to make an appointed time happen on your timetable.

Once these are in order, trust God to fulfill the desires He has placed in your heart in due season and allow desire to supernaturally order your race and propel you toward God's perfect plan for you.

CHAPTER 6

DESIRE AND *Decisions*

Desire is a powerful spiritual force, and as we have seen, it is a primary way in which God brings direction to a believer. Another important aspect of desire is that it has the power to produce consistent behavior in our lives.

When you think about it, it is an easy truth to understand. If you have a strong desire to do something, you tend to make decisions to devote your time and energy to the thing you desire the most.

On the other hand, you may set a goal, but you will not be consistent in your pursuit of your objective unless you have a strong desire for it. Why? Because desire is what gives you the determination and staying power to pursue a particular direction or goal.

The reality is that the things you desire most strongly and the things that burn most intensely in your heart are, ultimately, the things you decide to pursue with the most persistency. The most consistent decisions you make in a particular area are a product of the strongest desire you have regarding that area of your life.

In other words, you won't have strong desire and then make decisions opposite to that desire. That's not the way you were created to function. So it behooves us to understand specifically how the decision-making process is designed and how we can make the power of desire work for us.

God's Design for Decisions

The Bible teaches we are a spirit, we have a soul, and we live in a body. Our right to choose, our free moral agency, or our will is located in our soul. Now, very simply, your soul is comprised of your mind (what you think), your will (what you want), and your emotions (what you feel). And, essentially, what you think interacts with what you feel which produces desire. So, on a regular basis, when what you think interacts with what you feel, whichever between the two is most dominant will usually determine your decision. And thus, whatever is the dominant influence over your thoughts and feelings is controlling your decision-making process.

On one hand, your soul is being influenced through the desires of your body. Daily, Satan will use the carnal things of the world to bombard your senses in an effort to influence your soul.

And on the other hand, your recreated human spirit is being influenced by God to make decisions that will take you toward life and blessing. And this is really what spiritual warfare is all about—who can exercise the greatest influence on the decision-making process.

Ungodly influences usually manifest as pressure through adversity and difficult circumstance. Thus, don't ever make a decision to relieve the pressure as this will be a decision dictated by the wrong influence. On the other hand, God generates influence through the desire that burns within you. The more you can intensify that desire and the more you allow it to direct your choices, it will constrain your decision making to accommodate the will of God.

DECISIONS AND THE LAW OF THE MIND

So, ultimately, behavior is determined by the decision-making process of the soul. And this process operates under *the law of the mind* as revealed in Romans 7:22 where Paul says, "I delight in the law of God according to the inward man…" (NKJV). And then in verse 23 he says, "But I see another law in my members, warring against *the law of my mind,* and bringing me into captivity to the law of sin which is in my members" (NKJV).

The apostle Paul, inspired by the Holy Spirit, is pointing out the conflict that every Christian experiences. We hear and believe God's Word and begin to delight in it inwardly. Yet other influences are seeking to work through our flesh and limit the fruit-bearing potential of the seed that has been planted in our hearts.

The battle is waged in the realm of the soul, specifically the mind. And your ability to operate the law of the mind properly will determine which desires burn the most fervently in your heart.

Your mind works by mental imagery, meaning you don't think in words, you think in images. For example, if I said to you the words "yellow dog," you wouldn't see in your mind the letters y-e-l-l-o-w d-o-g. You would see a yellow dog—a picture, a mental image. That's the way the mind functions.

Some of your imagery comes through your eyes and other senses, but your mind has the ability to generate imagery that is independent of sensory input. Your mind is connected to and influenced by your natural senses, and it is influenced by your spirit, but you control your mind's imagery. You control your thoughts, and they can have a powerful influence on your desire.

If you meditate on something, your thoughts begin to generate a desire for that thing. Also meditation and speaking words are closely connected according to Joshua 1:8. We tend to talk about the things we think about and speaking elevates the intensity of desire. The more we talk about the things of God, the greater our desire for them becomes.

Hebrews 11:13-16 talks about heroes of faith who had embraced God's promises. They begin by speaking out and confessing the promises, and then they received desire. The point is the words we speak have a lot to do with what we think about and, thus, have an impact on desire.

DECISIONS AND OUR IMAGINATION

"If you can think it, you can do it," is an advertising slogan, but it is rooted in a spiritual truth. In 1 Peter 1:13, the apostle Peter makes a statement that gives us more insight into this matter: "Wherefore gird up the loins of your mind, be sober [that means sound minded], and hope [or confidently expect, talking about the promise of God] to the end for the grace that is to be brought unto you at the revelation of Jesus Christ."

In the first part of this verse, he says "gird up the loins of your mind." The word "loins" fascinates me. If you look it up in the dictionary, it means "the seat of procreative power." Now in a biological sense, our loins are located somewhere else. And it's the way biological life is conceived and brought into this natural arena. So obviously, he's talking about some other kind of life.

God has created your mind with the capacity to bring the life of God into manifestation in this natural arena. When you're born again, the life of God takes up residence on the inside of you. The challenge for the believer then is to turn spiritual truth into temporal truth. Somehow or some way, you have to get the spiritual truth that's on the inside of you out into the natural arena of life—and your mind is the key to making that happen.

Your mind has the power to bring the life that's inside of you out into a natural existence. That's why God refers to it as the loins of your mind. The capacity to produce life in the natural realm is in your mind.

Genesis 11, which is the biblical account of the Tower of Babel, illustrates the power of imagination. The people of Babel were an unregenerate people. Nevertheless, when God came down to see the city and the tower they built, He said, "Nothing they have imagined they can do will be impossible for them." It is a spiritual law. We will not be restrained from what we imagine we can do.

Certainly, there are times when you need to focus on the basics of day to day living, like balancing your checkbook or driving your car. But when you have discretionary thought time, you need to focus on the Lord. You need to think about the desires He has placed in your heart and the things He has promised you. Think about the magnitude and excitement of your heavenly rewards and your eternal destiny. Think about the great day when you meet Jesus face to face. Think about ruling and reigning with Him. Think about these things, and they will increase your desire for the Lord.

Renewing the Mind

When operated as God intends, the law of the mind will bring forth consistent behavior in line with the Word sown in your heart. Yet it's important to recognize that the law of the mind operates whether what you are trying to achieve is good or bad. Just like gravity, a law is a law and it works regardless of the circumstances or who is involved. In other words, the law of the mind is always at work whether a person realizes it or not.

Thus, in order to make consistent decisions which keep your life within the parameters of God's will for you, you need to go through a process called "renewing the mind." This process is described in Romans 12:2, which says, "And be not conformed to this world: but be ye transformed by the renewing of your mind, that ye may prove what is that good, and acceptable, and perfect will of God" (NKJV).

The Amplified Bible translates it even more clearly: "Do not be conformed to this world (this age), [fashioned after and adapted to its external, superficial customs], but be transformed (changed) by the [entire] renewal of your mind [by its new ideals and its new attitude], so that you may prove [for yourselves] what is the good and acceptable and perfect will of God, even the thing which is good and acceptable and perfect [in His sight for you]."

To be *transformed* means your mind has to be renewed. Even though Romans 12:2 is a familiar verse to most Christians, the actual process of renewing the mind and what it entails is not understood as it should be. If it was, we would see a whole lot more Christian butterflies than caterpillars!

Renewing isn't just learning or even memorizing Scripture. Renewing means refilling or replenishing. Renewing the mind is taking what you have already learned and doing something with it called refilling and replenishing, which is a continual act.

In the same way that faith comes by hearing and hearing and hearing, so does renewing the mind come by renewing and renewing and renewing. It is a continual process of refilling and replenishing your mind with things you've already learned.

It's an ongoing process and is initiated by two critical sources: God's written Word and what the Holy Spirit speaks to you personally. God wants you to replace what the world has programmed you to think with the paradigm of life that the Word of God gives you.

That process is called renewal. Renewal is the process of adopting an entire system of values, an entire way of looking at life from the Bible's perspective that flows in an opposite direction from the world's system of thinking and living.

God wants you to study, understand, and adopt His way of thinking and use it to replace what the world has taught you during your years on earth.

What to Renew Your Mind to First

The foundation upon which the entire renewal process is built is found in the words of

Jesus in John chapter 15:7: "If you abide in Me, and My words abide in you, you will ask what you desire, and it shall be done for you" (NKJV).

The word *abide* has broad application; it is another way of saying "delight in the Lord" like Psalm 37:4. It also certainly refers to what we do with our minds as the statement "My words abiding in you" indicates. Yet this passage also reveals foundationally what we must renew our minds to. "If you abide in me" comes first, thus abiding involves being consciously aware of the indwelling presence of God in your life.

This is a key part of the process for developing godly desire and making daily decisions which lead you toward your destiny. You must abide in Him which involves continually refilling and replenishing your conscious awareness of the presence of God in your life.

To experience transformation, you must become grounded (mentally renewed) in the fact that He never leaves you nor forsakes you. He's closer than your skin. He (the greater One) lives on the inside of you. You are the temple of the Holy Spirit. He goes with you wherever you go.

Wrong Desires Changed— Right Desires Fulfilled!

John 15:7 in the Wuest Bible translation reveals another aspect of what will be transformed as you truly abide and begin the process of renewing your mind as the Bible describes:

> *If you maintain a living communion with Me and My words are at home in you, then I command you to ask, at once, something for yourself whatever your heart desires and it will become yours.*

Isn't that awesome? He's saying that as you renew your mind and begin to maintain a conscious awareness of God's abiding presence, it is the foundation for your desires to be right and generated by the Holy Spirit. And then, when you ask something, it will automatically be in line with that desire and it will be yours.

The bottom line is this: if you become consciously aware and focus your thought life on the abiding presence of God, wrong desires will be changed and right desires will be generated that are in line with His will. And that makes it possible for God to say to you, "Ask. Do it now. Whatever things your heart desires, I can bring it to pass now."

Doesn't this bring Psalm 37:4 into perspective? Delighting yourself involves both abiding and using your mind. Delight is thinking. It's mentally imaging. It's meditating. It's getting your life in alignment with the Word. It's changing the way you see things.

When you delight yourself, you abide in Him and thus your desires are God given. You begin to analyze and evaluate every decision you face in light of the fire burning in your heart. You are consistently aware of the fact that He is always with you and never leaves you.

That means when you get a bad report on your physical health, instead of thinking, *Oh, I'm going to die,* you think, *The Healer lives in me.* That means when you hear the Holy Spirit tell you where to live, whom to marry, and so on, you'll recognize His voice. It won't be hard to figure out the will of God for your life and you'll know that's the way you're to go.

DECISIONS DIRECTED BY GODLY DESIRE

Certainly, God's plan can be much bigger than your own imagination, but when He gives you a glimpse of His design for your life, you need to trust your God-given desires.

As we spend time refining the things God has shown us, our thoughts elevate the level of our desire, and desire causes us to become determined. Desire causes us to become passionate. Desire and mental imagery work hand in hand to produce the direction of God for your life.

Your daily decisions will be directed by His desires and you will discover that your steps are somehow supernaturally ordered. Every day a new door opens and a new opportunity comes. The right people are in the right place at the right time, and each day moves you closer to God's unique plan for you.

Conclusion

Since the day I was born again, I have had the desire to be a man after God's own heart. This desire is something that God put into me. It gives momentum and excitement to my life. It is my greatest desire.

When you follow the desires of your heart, life takes on an exciting luster. You look forward to getting out of bed in the morning. Following your heart's desire generates momentum and orders your behavior in a positive way. It sets you on the path to a joyful, successful life.

Yet one of the saddest things I have observed about our society is that a huge segment of America's population has no meaningful desire. Often, people's greatest desire is to have a nice evening after spending the day at a job they don't enjoy. We've all heard people say, "I'm just working for the weekend."

It is a fact that weak desire produces insignificant accomplishment. The tragedy is that many people who have a lot of potential are squandering their opportunities in life because they lack desire.

Even when convinced about the importance of desire and what the Bible has to say about it, many Christians have a hard time believing that God directs them by giving them desires.

They know their own weaknesses and past mistakes and realize their flesh is capable of producing desires that lead them into sin, so they are cautious about desire. They are so afraid of following wrong desire that they don't trust their God-given desires and don't give an important place to them.

Of course, if the desire is rooted primarily in self-gratification, you probably should disregard it. However, if you can truthfully say that you have put God first place in your life, if you have diligently sought God and delighted in Him, you need to trust the desire that comes.

Why? Because whether it's the shape and the nature of our eternal experience, whether it's the level of blessing and fulfillment we receive now in this life, whether it's being part of something that is highly effective or modestly mediocre, everything depends on whether or not we become impassioned and stirred about what we do.

Thus, I encourage you to recognize the important role desire plays in your daily life, understand the position desire plays in lighting your way, and thus begin as never before to pay attention to the desires of your heart.

To clarify your calling, to discover your destiny, to fulfill the will of God for your life, you must follow the fire of desire that burns in your heart!

Prayer of Salvation

A born-again, committed relationship with God is the key to a victorious life. Jesus, the Son of God, laid down His life and rose again so that we could spend eternity with Him in heaven and experience His absolute best on earth. The Bible says, "For God so loved the world, that he gave his only begotten Son, that whosoever believeth in him should not perish, but have everlasting life" (John 3:16).

It is the will of God that everyone receive eternal salvation. The way to receive this salvation is to call upon the name of Jesus and confess Him as your Lord. The Bible says, "That if thou shalt confess with thy mouth the Lord Jesus, and shalt believe in thine heart that God hath raised him from the dead, thou shalt be saved. For whosoever shall call upon the name of the Lord shall be saved" (Romans 10:9, 13).

Jesus has given salvation, healing, and countless benefits to all who call upon His name. These benefits can be yours if you receive Him into your heart by praying this prayer:

Heavenly Father, I come to You admitting that I am a sinner. Right now, I choose to turn away from sin, and I ask You to cleanse me of all unrighteousness. I believe that Your Son, Jesus, died on the cross to take away my sins.

I also believe that He rose again from the dead so that I may be justified and made righteous through faith in Him. I call upon the name of Jesus Christ to be the Savior and Lord of my life. Jesus, I choose to follow You, and I ask that You fill me with the power of the Holy Spirit. I declare right now that I am a born again child of God. I am free from sin and full of the righteousness of God. I am saved in Jesus' name, amen.

If you have just received Jesus Christ as your Savior, or if this book has changed your life, we would like to hear from you. Please write us at:

Mac Hammond Ministries
PO Box 29469
Minneapolis, Minnesota 55429-2946

You can also visit us on the web at
mac-hammond.org.

About The Author

Mac Hammond is senior pastor of Living Word Christian Center, a large and growing body of Christian believers in Brooklyn Park (a suburb of Minneapolis), Minnesota. He is the host of the *Winner's Way* broadcast and author of several internationally distributed books. Mac is broadly acclaimed for his ability to apply the principles of the Bible to practical situations and the challenges of daily living.

Mac Hammond graduated from Virginia Military Institute in 1965 with a Bachelor's degree in English. Upon graduation, he entered the Air Force with a regular officer's commission and reported for pilot training at Moody Air Force Base in Georgia. He received his wings in November 1966, and subsequently served two tours of duty in Southeast Asia, accumulating 198 combat missions. He was honorably discharged in 1970 with the rank of Captain.

Between 1970 and 1980, Mac was involved in varying capacities in the general aviation industry including ownership of a successful air cargo business serving the Midwestern United States. A business acquisition brought the Hammonds to Minneapolis where they ultimately founded Living Word Christian Center in 1980 with 12 people in attendance.

After more than 27 years, that group of twelve people has grown into an active church body of more than 9,000 members. Today some of the outreaches that spring from Living Word include Maranatha Christian Academy, a fully-accredited, pre-K through 12th grade Christian school; Maranatha College, an evening college with an uncompromising Christian environment; Living Free Recovery Services, a state licensed outpatient treatment facility for chemical dependency; The Wells at 7th Street, a multi-faceted outreach to inner-city residents; CFAITH, an online cooperative missionary outreach of hundreds of national and international organizations providing faith-based content; and a national and international media outreach that includes hundreds of audio/video teaching series, the *Winner's Way* broadcast, the *PrayerNotes* newsletter, and the *Winner's Way* magazine.

Other Books

By Mac Hammond

Angels at Your Service
   Releasing the Power of Heaven's Host

Doorways to Deception
   How Deception Comes, How It Destroys, and How You Can Avoid It

Heirs Together
   Solving the Mystery of a Satisfying Marriage

The Last Millennium
   A Revealing Look at the Remarkable Days Ahead and How You Can Live Them to the Fullest

Living Safely in a Dangerous World
   Keys to Abiding in the Secret Place

Plugged In and Prospering
   Embracing the Spiritual Significance and Biblical Basis for the Local Church

Positioned for Promotion
   How to Increase Your Influence and Capacity to Lead

Real Faith Never Fails
   Detecting (and Correcting) Four Common Faith Mistakes

By Mac Hammond (continued)

Simplifying Your Life
   Divine Insights to Uncomplicated Living

Soul Control
   Whoever Controls Your Soul, Controls Your Destiny

Water, Wind, & Fire
   Understanding the New Birth and the Baptism of the Holy Spirit

Water, Wind, & Fire—The Next Steps
   Developing Your New Relationship With God

The Way of the Winner
   Running the Race to Victory

Who God Is Not
   Exploding the Myths About His Nature and His Ways

Winning In Your Finances
   How to Walk God's Pathway to Prosperity

Winning Your World
   Becoming a Person of Influence

Yielded and Bold
   How to Understand and Flow With the Move of God's Spirit

By Mac and Lynne Hammond

Keys to Compatibility
Opening the Door to a Marvelous Marriage

By Lynne Hammond

Dare to Be Free!

Heaven's Power for the Harvest
Be Part of God's End-Time Spiritual Outpouring

Living in the Presence of God
Receive Joy, Peace, and Direction in the Secret Place of Prayer

Love and Devotion
Prayer Journal

The Master Is Calling
Discovering the Wonders of Spirit-Led Prayer

The Master Is Calling Workbook
Discovering the Wonders of Spirit-Led Prayer

By Lynne Hammond (continued)

Renewed in His Presence
Satisfying Your Hunger for God

Secrets to Powerful Prayer
Discovering the Languages of the Heart

Staying Faith
How to Stand Until the Answer Arrives

The Table of Blessing
Recipes From the Family and Friends of Living Word Christian Center

When Healing Doesn't Come Easily

When It's Time for a Miracle
The Hour of Impossible Breakthroughs Is Now!

Whispers From the Secret Place
A 31-day Journey

For a complete catalog of our books, CDs, and DVDs, please contact us at:

Mac Hammond Ministries
PO Box 29469
Minneapolis, Minnesota 55429-2946

You can also visit us on the web at
mac-hammond.org.